Journey to Praise

# "JOURNEY to PRAISE"

A
  Book
    of
      Consecration
        and
          Fasting

## Jackie Dotson

# Journey to Praise

Unless otherwise indicated, Scripture verses are taken from the King James Version.

Verses marked NKJV are Scriptures taken from the New King James Version®. Copyright © 1982 by Thomas Nelson. Used by permission. All rights reserved.

Verses marked NIV are taken from THE HOLY BIBLE, NEW INTERNATIONAL VERSION®, NIV® Copyright © 1973, 1978, 1984, 2011 by Biblica, Inc.® Used by permission. All rights reserved worldwide.

Verses marked NET are taken from the New English Translation. NET Bible® copyright ©1996-2006 by Biblical Studies Press, L.L.C. http://netbible.com . All rights reserved.

Cover *by*:

**"JOURNEY to Praise"** – **A Book of Consecration and Fasting**
Copyright © 2015 by: Jackie Dotson
Published by: God's Divine Journey, LLC
P.O Box 1572, Kennesaw, GA 30156
Godsdivinejourneyllc@gmail.com
**ISBN 9780692351024 (pbk color)**
**All rights reserved**. No part of this publication may be reproduced, stored in a retrieval system, or transmitted in any form or by any means—electronic, mechanical, digital, photocopy, recording, or any other—except for brief quotations in printed reviews, without the prior permission of the publisher. **Printed in the United States of America.**

# Journey to Praise

## DEDICATION

I would like to dedicate this book to the love of my life, the True and Living God, my Savior, my Jehovah. Thank You, Lord, for saving me. Thank You, Lord, for directing me. Thank You, Lord, for working with me. Thank You, Lord, for working through me. Thank You, Lord, for healing me. Thank You, Lord, for using me as a vessel for Your Glory. Thank You, Lord, for allowing me to go on this magnificent journey with You, so I can share Your Power and Your Word with the world.

I give God all the praise for my mother, Lillian; father, Haskell; grandmother, Mama Heard, and great aunt, Mama Sparks, for introducing me to God the Father, the Son, and the Holy Spirit from the beginning of my life. I am grateful to them for allowing their light to shine, so that others could see the Jesus in them.

## Special Thanks

Thank you to my cousin, Cherry, for inspiring me to write down my experience, and going through this journey with me. Thank you to Andre, my nephew, my baby, who endured part of this journey with me, and was blessed with increased faith through it. Thank you to my sister, Karen, for encouraging me to turn this journey into a book, and to my sister, Rose, for echoing Karen's encouragement. Thank you both for helping with the editing and layout of this book.

Thank you Dorothy, my dear friend, and adopted sister, for helping me edit and publish this tool (you were truly God sent). To my close friend, Tony, thank you for letting God use you to encourage me, for not letting me give up when I wanted to, and for allowing God to use you to not let me fall. Thanks to my Pastors, who let God use them as divine direction in my life. Thank you all, may God continue to bless, keep and use each one of you to His Glory. I love you.

# Journey to Praise

**He is Worthy to be Praised.................**

O come, let us sing unto the LORD: let us make a joyful noise to the rock of our salvation.

Let us come before his presence with thanksgiving, and make a joyful noise unto him with psalms.

For the LORD *is* a great God, and a great King above all gods.

In his hand *are* the deep places of the earth: the strength of the hills *is* his also.

The sea *is* his, and he made it: and his hands formed the dry *land*.

O come, let us worship and bow down: let us kneel before the LORD our maker.

For he *is* our God; and we *are* the people of his pasture, and the sheep of his hand. Today if ye will hear his voice,

Harden not your heart, as in the provocation, *and* as *in* the day of temptation in the wilderness:

When your fathers tempted me, proved me, and saw my work.

Forty years long was I grieved with *this* generation, and said, It *is* a people that do err in their heart, and they have not known my ways:

Unto whom I sware in my wrath that they should not enter into my rest.

**Psalms 95:1-11**

# Journey to Praise

## Contents

1. Introduction……………………………………..…..8
   - My Story………………………………………..10
   - My Journey…………………………….......12
   - What does Consecration & Fasting Mean?............................16

2. My Journey to Praise……………………….…..22

3. Journey after My 21 Day Fast……………40

4. Your Journey to Praise………………..……..53

5. Journey Continues……………………….…123

# Journey to Praise

## Praising Changes Our Lives.....................

God be merciful unto us, and bless us; *and* cause his face to shine upon us; Selah.

That thy way may be known upon earth, thy saving health among all nations.

Let the people praise thee, O God; let all the people praise thee.

O let the nations be glad and sing for joy: for thou shalt judge the people righteously, and govern the nations upon earth. Selah.

Let the people praise thee, O God; let all the people praise thee.

*Then* shall the earth yield her increase; *and* God, *even* our own God, shall bless us.

God shall bless us; and all the ends of the earth shall fear him.

**Psalms 67:1-7**

## Journey to Praise

## INTRODUCTION

What do you need from God right now? Do you find yourself feeling hopeless, depressed, and disgusted with the challenges that life brings? Maybe, you have even considered suicide or physically harming someone else. Are you in the middle of a test that just doesn't seem to end?

Well, back in year 2012, that is how I found myself feeling, but the grace of God, changed my life and turned my situation around. During this period, God spoke to me and asked, "Are you using the tools, in which, I have given you?" This is when I realized that sometimes God will allow for a challenging situation to enter into our lives, just to get our attention and to get us closer to Him. I'm a witness to God taking a bad situation, changing it completely and using it to His good; just like He did with Joseph in the Bible (Genesis 50:20).

Throughout my journey, God revealed His power in the significance of the number

# Journey to Praise

**three**.  As you read this book, you will see how <u>the Father</u>, <u>the Son</u> and <u>the Holy Spirit</u> **(three)** show up in a mighty way.
 Hallelujah! Hallelujah! Hallelujah!

## My Story

My life was just going crazy! The enemy had been beating me down for six consecutive years. The first **three** years, I was challenged with my health and the next **three** years, I was dragged down by my finances. You know, these two tests/problems can put you in a state of depression, destroying self-confidence, feeling purposeless and not wanting to keep pressing forward.

You see, God was healing my body from what doctors diagnosed me with, multiple sclerosis (MS), and I was praising Him for His loving kindness and His grace during this first test. However, before I could get out of the first test completely, I found myself in another one. Satan appeared in person and came as a self-proclaimed minister; just as the Word speaks of the devil coming in His name (Matthew 7:15), this man approached me. This individual scammed me, I found myself without credit and I almost lost my home. I was in a very deep valley during this season of my life. I found myself feeling depressed and feeling useless. The

## Journey to Praise

depression was so deep, I thought about ending my life. I didn't want to face the embarrassment of failure. This is when the Lord, our Savior, took me on a journey to get closer to Him; journeys to start using me to His glory, by letting me know it was not about me, **It Was All About Him.**

Have you ever had God tell you to do something that just didn't make sense to you at the time (something crazy)? Well, that is exactly what happened to me. I didn't understand it, but I did it anyway. I was obedient and He revealed His grace. Sometimes, we just have to take that step of faith and it will take you/us to a whole new level. God wants to take us to higher heights and deeper depths in Him. Praise God!

# Journey to Praise

## My Journey

This is how the journey started. I was a member of a well known church, but I felt I needed more. I found myself seeking and searching for a church that would help me in my spiritual growth. Sometimes, we find ourselves searching, but looking in all the wrong places. Places that are not of God.

Have you ever felt desperate, lost and/or hopeless? This is when you have an opportunity to make some changes in your life. My strength came from the love I have for the Lord, even though Satan was trying to destroy me. By listening to that still small voice inside of me (the Holy Spirit), I sought God first.

I always had a relationship with the Lord, but this time it was different. I sought Him on this journey with more praise and more obedience. I just wanted to hear from Him, and was hoping He would just snap His fingers, and make everything in my life okay. You see, I was desperate; I was even

## Journey to Praise

willing to give up my hard-earned week of vacation, just to spend it with the Lord. This is when God showed me I had to first seek and trust Him, be more patience, make spiritual changes in my life, and use His Word as a tool to guide me. He showed me that the victory was already mine. I just had to tap into it through Him.

I ended up visiting a church with a Pentecostal background. This is a church that is spirit-led, crazy for God, believes in praising, praising, praising Him, and doesn't have a problem showing its enthusiasm and excitement for God. This was a whole new experience for me, because I grew up in a church denomination that was much quieter and more laid-back. Even so, with this overwhelming change, I fell in love with my newly found church. I started attending service every Sunday. I then started going on Wednesday evenings for bible study and eventually, I was at prayer service every Saturday. This was the beginning of the realization of my calling and venture into fulfilling my purpose, which God always had for me.

## Journey to Praise

As you read this book, you will see that when you seek God first, He will fix the broken pieces, and replace whatever is missing in your life (Matthew 6:33). In fact, He will direct you on how to do these things yourself through His power. Yes, He has given us authority to use His tools. He will show you His way, His truth, and His life (John 14:6).

This book is the chronicle of a one year journey, which God took me on to turn my life around. However, God never does anything little; He does it big, for He is the Almighty and the all Powerful God (**El Shaddai**). The journey He took me on, as you will see, was filled with trials and tests. During this time, God used me to touch and speak to other people, and to help put them on the path on which He placed me on (a path to a life of victory). He was not only fixing my problems, He was fixing problems of others in my life, and now, He wants to fix your problems.

Continue to read on and dig deep into this book, using it as a tool to experience a supernatural life changing season. God has set all of us up for victory in and through Him; His Word is true and all we have to do is stand on His promises. However, we must first read His Word to know what His promises are for us. Many of us read His Word as if it was for the past and not for today. **Miracles, signs, and wonders** are still available for us today. We must believe in order to receive, and do what is pleasing in His sight (John 14:15-30).

This book will open your eyes up to the power of consecration. The Bible speaks of Jesus telling His disciples that some things take more than prayer; they must also fast (Matthew 17:21).

## What does consecration and fasting mean?

**Consecration:** According to the *Online Dictionary*, consecration means "to declare or set apart as sacred for a holy use to dedicate solemnly to God. To dedicate (one's life, time, etc) to a specific purpose for God." My definition of consecration is to go on a vacation <u>totally</u> with God.

**Fasting and prayer:** According to the Online Website ***allaboutprayer.org*** Prayer and fasting is defined as, "Voluntarily going without food in order to focus on prayer and fellowship with God. Prayer and fasting often go hand in hand, but this is not always the case. However, it is when these two activities are combined and dedicated to God's glory that they reach their full effectiveness. It is simply forcing yourself to focus and rely on God for the strength, provision, and wisdom you need." My definition of prayer and fasting, is to stay in communication with God for a certain period of time (hours, or days), and giving up

## Journey to Praise

something very dear to you like a food, all food, or an activity that would be hard for you to give up. Remember, you are sacrificing unto the Lord, and using the tools.

God wants you to totally submit and dedicate yourself to Him; having that quiet time, so you can hear Him speak to you. In order to see God, you must have your ears open to Him. We only see God through hearing Him speak to us, and then seeing Him make provisions in our lives. Yes, it's the Holy Spirit who lives in us.

Also, you will see it is true that **obedience** is the key to tapping into what God has for you. God may have you do something you think you cannot do (crazy)! However, He will guide you and see you through it all. He will reward you for your obedience abundantly and exceedingly (1 Samuel 15:22). This is when the chains will be broken, breakthroughs occur, strongholds are broken and God's overflow comes knocking at your door.

## Journey to Praise

We must not forget that <u>prayer</u> (a tool) is essential in our lives, and we should do it in our prayer closet (Matthew 6:6). We must also have prayer partners and do it corporately, as there is power in <u>praying in numbers</u> (Matthew 18:19). It is so important for us to read God's Word, have a relationship with Him, and stand on His Word (the Truth). It is through hearing and reading His Word that strengthens our <u>faith</u>, another tool (Romans 10:17). Also, reading <u>His Word</u> (yet, another tool), tells us how to handle every situation in our lives.

I will share with you my story of consecrating myself for a seven day period, and of how my radical obedience for one year changed my life, and redirected my path according to God's will. As mentioned earlier, God spoke to me telling me, "We do not use the tools, in which, He has given us."

Following my story, is a daily layout of praises and scriptures for you to use as a guide and tool for your twenty-one day fast. Start preparing a time that you will set apart just for God and you - a vacation. Also,

## Journey to Praise

included at the end of this book, is a special bonus. Get ready for **the Heavenly Father!** Get ready for **the Son, Jesus!** Get ready for **the Holy Spirit, the Comforter!**

I pray this book will change your life, so that you will never be the same. I pray this book will be an eye opener to God's power. I pray you will see the importance of praise, prayer, tithing, reading God's Word, gifts of the spirit, fruits of the spirit, putting on the full armor of God and fasting.

When you seek God first, He will take care of all of your problems. In fact, I know if you use the tools that God has given you, your life will change, and you will not be the same. He will lift you up even during your trials and tribulations as long as your body, soul, and mind are fixed on Him. God will have you shine even in your darkness (2 Corinthians 4:6). He will give you His perfect peace and joy (Romans 15:13). Hallelujah! Hallelujah! Hallelujah! Praise His Holy Name!!!

## Journey to Praise

**Come on, let's get started. God has greatness just waiting for you. It is time to tap in now.**

Let us pray together as you enter into this book (a tool), and into my life changing experience, and your journey to praise!

### Prayer

*Dear Heavenly Father, we love You, Lord. We thank You, Lord, for loving us so much. Thank You, Lord, for Your loving kindness, for Your mercy and Your grace. Father, thank You, Lord, for sending Your precious Son and sacrificing Him, so that we may have eternal life. What a precious gift. Hallelujah! Oh God, we come humbly before You right now, asking You to cleanse each and every one of us of our sins, Father. We repent right now. Lord God, we ask that my journey of praise can be a beacon of light for others to help them to get closer to You. Let this journey touch them, so that whatever they are going through they know it is not too big for You, because You are almighty and all powerful. Oh God, we thank You in advance for what You are going to do, and how You are going to touch and change all who tap into the tools You have for them. Use each and every one of us for Your Glory. We Praise You, Lord! We Glorify Your Holy Name! In Jesus Name we pray. Amen! Amen! Amen!*

# Journey to Praise

> *But the hour cometh, and now is, when the true worshipers shall worship the Father in spirit and in truth: for the Father seeketh such to worship him.*
>
> *John 4:23*

## My Journey to Praise

My Consecration and Fast
July 30, 2012- August 19, 2012
(Twenty-one days)

On July 21, 2012, I went for a two hour walk with my dog, Romeo, and during this time, I meditated on God. I knew in a week I would be on a one week vacation from work. So, I asked God, "What am I going to do on my vacation?" I thought maybe I would go home to Milwaukee, WI, for a week, but God spoke to me and said, "Spend your vacation with me and consecrate yourself." I said to Him, "Okay, God. How do you want me to do that?" He told me, "Shut yourself in your house with Me, disconnect the home phone, and tell your family and friends not to call."

He further told me, "Watch religious programs on TV that will allow you to focus only on Me." He directed me to spend all of my time praising Him, praying to Him, reading His Word, worshiping Him, and reading self-help books about Him (using

## Journey to Praise

His tools). My instructions also included, walking daily for two hours; but while walking, I needed to meditate and praise Him.

Also, I was invited to take communion every day in the morning, and fast by eating only fruits and vegetables (no starchy veggies). I would only be around people when I went to Church on Wednesday, Friday, Saturday and Sunday. You see, God will tell you just what He wants you to do, how to do it, and you will hear Him, because His sheep hear His voice (John 10:27). My house became filled with God's presence 24/7. It was amazing! My house was a sanctuary. It was the best trip and vacation I have ever gone on. Praise God! Hallelujah! Hallelujah! Hallelujah!

On Sunday, July 29, 2012, I went to the grocery store after church and bought my food for the fast. I was so excited to get started, but at the same time, I was scared that I couldn't do it, and that I would not stick with it. Satan tried to creep in, but I rebuked him. I looked up to the hills, to our

## Journey to Praise

Savior, and asked for His divine help, and I pressed forward (Psalms 121:1). The next day, I started my "Praise Fast" and prayer. I was on my Journey to Praise.

I went into my home office and pulled every book that was about God (over **30** books) out of my bookcase, and took them all to my bedroom, where I spread them on my floor. All the while, I was asking God which book should I start reading first, and He lead me to a book on prayer, so during that week, I read **three** books on prayer. I did not know why God gave me these books to read, but later, He revealed it to me, and it was greater than what I could have even imagined. He was preparing me and turning me into a prayer warrior for others and myself. Until this experience, I just didn't quite understand the power of prayer, now I pray for everything. I know prayer is very powerful, and it changes things when we go to God in the name of Jesus (John 14:13-14).

The first two days, I praised God, worshiped Him, prayed and did everything that He told

## Journey to Praise

me to do. For example, on the second day, God told me to give. I went into my closet, packed everything I had available to give, which happened to be **three** bags of clothing and shoes. I immediately took them to a homeless shelter. God was first showing me, that it is better to give than to receive (Acts 20:35). It is in our giving that brings in the harvest (Isaiah 58:1-12).

Please note, this was my first time consecrating myself like this, and I had people mentioning to me that God will speak to you in a way that He never had in the past, so I waited. At first, I heard very little, but I told God, "I'm not stopping." However, on the **third** day, God started speaking to me, just pouring out His instructions to me. He told me to get a prayer partner, and He let me know that it should be my cousin, Cherry, in Georgia. I asked God, "Are You sure? Why do You not want me to ask my sisters?" I reminded myself that at the beginning of the week, I had spoken to God, and said, I would be obedient to whatever He told me to do.

## Journey to Praise

I called my cousin Cherry, who was surprised to hear from me, because I had mentioned, I would not be talking to her that week. I shared with her what God had given me to do. She was so humbled. She thanked God for selecting her, and we started to pray together that day. She then joined me on my seven day "Praise Fast." I shared with her the **three** things God gave me for prayer partnership: (1) God wanted us to write down a list of everything for which we each wanted prayer (2) We should collectively decide, touching and agreeing, what we would ask in prayer (3) We should pray together for one month (Habakkuk 2:2).

Each day, as we prayed together, the devil would interrupt our phone call and we would be disconnected. We had to rebuke Satan daily. Cherry and I found ourselves calling each other back several times to complete our prayer. Satan had a problem with what we were doing, and as we know when he is threatened, we know we are on the right track. Cherry and I just kept on persevering and praying without ceasing.

## Journey to Praise

We both knew where our help cometh from. In God's Word, He speaks of us coming to Him fervently without ceasing; so we decided to stand on His Word (1 Thessalonians 5:16-18). God was opening my eyes up to the power of praying in numbers, and fervently praying. I cannot even tell you of all the miracles, signs and wonders, we experienced daily; but I will attempt to, because it was simply amazing.

On the fourth day, God continued to speak to me and He placed it heavily on my heart; healing is in the name of Jesus (Mark 16: 17-18) and that there is healing for one of my cousins, who had a chronic illness. He told me to call her and pray for her. He gave me **three** things for her to do daily: (1) Praise God first thing in the morning upon awakening, (2) Read His Word, and (3) Thank Him for the Victory. After God gave me this message, I went for my two hour walk with Romeo, and I just praised God for what He had given me.

About 20 minutes into my walk, I looked behind me and saw a man with a slight limp

## Journey to Praise

approaching me. I looked back again and later crossed the street to get into some shade; I knew I had a long walk ahead of me. The Lord spoke to me and said, "Go back across the street and tell this man that I have healing for him, and that healing is In the Name of Jesus." Again, I questioned God and asked, "Do I have to, Lord? This man is going to think I'm crazy, Lord!" Then I told Him, "Yes, I will be obedient to Your commands." So, I crossed back over to the other side of the street and waited for the man to approach where I was standing. I asked him, "Do you believe in Jesus?" He replied, "Yes" and I went on to tell him that there was healing for him In the Name of Jesus. He looked astonished, but he thanked me. I went back across the street and continued my walk, now feeling a boldness that I never felt before.

During my walk, God continued to speak to me and He told me, I needed to anoint my nephew, Andre, in **the name of the Father, the Son and the Holy Spirit.** He also instructed me, to tell all of my family and friends to get prayer partners and fast on

## Journey to Praise

Wednesdays. I texted my nephew and told him what God wanted me to do. I felt a bit weird doing this, but I had to comply with God's will. To my surprise, Andre agreed and asked, "When?" He informed me that he would try to get to me, as soon as he could, because he did not have a car.

On Sunday, day fourteen of my extended fast, I picked up Andre and brought him to my house. I prayed over him and anointed him with the holy water that I had kept in my home for years. Here is one of my praise reports; God is now doing something special in my nephew's life. My family is now seeing breakthroughs, strongholds have been broken off of his life and he is now receiving God's divine overflow. Praise God!

Let's go back to day four. Later that evening, in obedience to God, I called my cousin who God wanted me to pray for healing. I really felt somewhat "weird" about calling her, because I wasn't known for calling people to pray with or for them. I wasn't known as a prayer warrior, yet, so I did not know how she would react towards my actions. However, she was receptive, so we prayed and we had a Hallelujah time on the phone. My Cousin thanked me, and I shared with her the **three** things that God had instructed me to give her. She, wholeheartedly said, she would do them.

A year later, I spoke with her, she told me that God was healing her and that this time it is different; it is spiritual. Praise His Holy name! Another year later, the Lord had taken my cousin home to be with Him. She is now whole with no more pain or sorrow.

Eternal life, with God, is what we all are looking forward to; as God sent His only son Jesus Christ to die on the cross for our sins, and He rose on the third day (1 Corinthians 15:4). So, as long as we believe in our Savior, and the sacrificing of His life for our sins, we will receive everlasting life with God Almighty (1 John 5:1-5). Hallelujah! God also showed me, we never know what the individual, whom we are praying for, is praying for himself or herself. I'm not sure what my cousin's prayers were, however, I

## Journey to Praise

know she loved the Lord, had faith and trusted Him.

Friday, the fifth day, God spoke to me and told me to call my family and friends. I was obedient; I started by calling my sisters and asked them to get prayer partners and to fast on Wednesdays.

Saturday, day six, I woke up, praised God and I was so full of the Holy Spirit, that before I left out for my walk, God immediately started speaking to me. He sat me down and gave me a Word to tell the church where I was attending. He told me to tell the Pastors, "Teach your members how to pray, since not everyone knows how to do this well." God also wanted me to inform them, "You need to fast as a church on Wednesdays, for the revival of My church." He indicated, "The church is going to have a revival that is going to be great; a huge revival, bigger and better than what you could ever imagine!" Again, I asked God, "Do You really want me to do this? The Pastors are going to think I'm seriously crazy. I'm not even a member of the church." Then I told God, "Okay, I will do it." Throughout this journey I said, I would be obedient to His request, no matter how out of character it would be for me.

Later, Romeo and I went out for our walk. About 15 minutes into the walk, I ran into the same gentleman who God told me on Thursday to speak of, "Healing In the Name of Jesus." He stopped and asked me, "Do you remember me?" I answered, "Yes." At that moment, he looked directly into my eyes and asked, **"What shall I do?"** When he asked me with those four words, I knew it was biblical - like a moment straight from the Bible. I told him the **three** things that God had given me to give my cousin for her healing. (1) Praise God when you get up and do not complain, (2) Read His Word, and (3) Thank Him for the Victory. He said, "Okay. I need a job. What shall I do?" I told him, "Everything is in the name of Jesus; He is a Provider, a Healer, a Protector, a Deliverer and a Redeemer."

When I was getting ready to leave he started bowing towards me as if I was the Lord,

## Journey to Praise

and I told him, "Please don't. I'm not God. I'm not even a minister. I'm just a servant for the Lord." He thanked me. I saw this man at least **three** more times, and God always used him as a sign telling me, everything is going to be okay. Thank You God!

On day seven, Sunday, I praised God, for it was my last day, but I didn't really want this vacation to end. Oh, what a glorious time I was having with Him! God had spoken to me all week (always while I was praising Him, and each time I heard His voice, His presence brought me to tears), telling me, **"We do not use the tools that He has given us: fasting, praying, reading His Word, speaking things into existence, walking in His authority, praise/worship, gifts/fruits of the spirit and putting on His full armor."** Also, God spoke to me telling me, the things we ask for are too little; we must start asking for what we think is the impossible **(BIG)**, because nothing is impossible or too **BIG** for Him!

God kept telling me at least five times on five different days, *that as long as we do*

***what is pleasing in His sight, follow His commandments and read His Word; He would give us our heart's desires.*** Prior to starting this consecration, I was reading the New Testament, starting with the first book Matthew, and reading it sequentially. It was so amazing. I was in the book of John at the start of this fast and God would end my readings with this <u>powerful</u> message on <u>five different days</u>. John speaks of this Word, five different times in the Bible. The number five is so significant, because, biblically, the number five is God giving us His grace and that is exactly what He was giving me.

God taught me how to truly seek Him during these seven days. During this consecration, He taught me how to be successful for the rest of my life. Our success is in seeking Him. He taught me that Praise, Praise, and more Praise brings God near, and that it changes things!!! We cannot be in God's presence and have things stay the same.

## Journey to Praise

During this fast, I asked Him, "How can I have the kind of faith that Peter had to walk on water?" God told me, "Look to Me and not the problem" (Matthew 14:29). Now, I live by looking to Him for everything no matter what the situation, good or bad. God is the master of changing a bad situation into a good thing. We must let the Holy Spirit guide us in all that we do. Hallelujah! Hallelujah! Hallelujah!

Oh yes, I was obedient! Radically, Obedient! Sunday, while at church, I spoke with the secretary and told her I had a Word for the Pastors. She told me to email them, so on the next day, I sent them this email:

Hello Pastors:

My name is Jackie Dotson and I'm not a member at your church yet; however, I have faithfully been attending since March of this year. I'm growing in my relationship with God through your spiritual leadership. To help you to remember me, I'm the young lady who had the card board testimony of being diagnosed with MS.

Okay, enough about me, this email is about the Grace of God and how He had spoken to me this

## Journey to Praise

past week while I was on vacation. A week prior to my vacation during my two hour walk on Saturday, I asked the Lord, "What am I going to do on my vacation." He said "Spend it with Me. Consecrate yourself." So, I was obedient, fasting and praying for seven days. During this time God spoke to me like He had never done before. In addition, I asked God to use me as a vessel for His Glory and I will be obedient.

Pastors, you asked us to pray for the both of you, so I started praying for you and for the church. I prayed for the church to have a revival. Saturday, during my consecration I was in the house praising God and He sat me down and started talking to me; giving this message for you:

1. The Lord told me to tell you to have the Church fast and pray every Wednesday for revival and He is going to give it to you. It is going to be bigger and greater than what you can even imagine. He said many souls will be saved during this revival.

2. Also, He said to teach your congregation how to pray because many of the members do not know how to pray and we must all be on one accord during this praying and fasting.

Just to let you know I'm usually a shy person, but I have been praying and asking God to make me more bold. Also, on Sunday when Pastor started singing and having the church sing "I will do what God tells me to do," that was just confirmation that

# Journey to Praise

I must be obedient and share this with you. If you would like to speak to me concerning this I would be glad to talk with you. ***I use an acronym to help people learn how to pray: P=Praise Him, R= Repent to Him, A=Ask Him and Y=Yield to Him.*** This may be something you can use to simplify prayer for the members of the Church. My prayer is for God to continue to bless both of you and to lift you up, all to His Glory. Praise God.

Jackie Dotson

**The Pastors responded back that they were very blessed with hearing from me and that it was just confirmation in what they were already hearing.**

After the seventh day of my consecration, I shared with other family and friends the message God had given me. God just spoke to me at the end of my fast saying, "People all over the world would be fasting and praying on Wednesdays. If done corporately, breakthroughs, breaking strongholds (chains and bondage falling off of us) and overflow (e.g. in our health, our finances, dreams) will occur in our lives." Praise Be to God, The Most High! I can truly say by Cherry's and my **obedience**, we are continually receiving God's abundant blessings in our lives. Thank You God!

As my journey continued, the Lord first spoke to my Cousin, Cherry, telling her to have us fast 14 days. He then told me for us to do it 21 days (**three weeks**), and we were **obedient**. My vacation from work ended, but we still continued with our 21 day fast. We fasted together for the entire 21 days, and we prayed together for the whole month as God had instructed us to do, missing only one day of prayer. God truly blessed us through these 21 days and a month of seeking Him. We both found God's peace and His perfect joy. Cherry and I had been hit financially, but God gave us peace even during these trials. Hallelujah! Hallelujah! Hallelujah!

# Journey to Praise

> *But whosoever drinketh of the water that I shall give him shall never thirst; but the water that I shall give him shall be in him a well of water springing up into everlasting life.*
>
> *John 4:14*

## Journey after the 21 Day Fast

God spoke to Cherry and me, and we listened. He instructed us to continue praying and fasting together for one year. During that one year, we fasted together on Wednesdays for several months and prayed daily, missing only a few days. In addition, we fasted 21 days in January, 2013, coupled with several seven and **three** day fasts. We simply just started tapping into God's power, the power that He has given us the authority to use, His tools (Luke 9:1).

God answered so many of our prayers, including: (1) He used us to intercede for people who were ill. (2) He sent us our Boazes (Ruth 2). (3) Miraculously, He sent us new cars. One car was received after a **three** day fast (we call it the "Hallelujah Car"), and the other was taken back from the enemy (this car we call "In God We Trust Car"). How thankful we are to God! (4) He made my mortgage and other bills more affordable. (5) He turned my job situation around for the good (Romans 8:28).

## Journey to Praise

(6) He started an entrepreneur business for one of my nephews and four of his college friends. A famous star provided finances and located their business in an exclusive area, what a blessing! (7) He started restoring our families. You know God has a sense of humor. He can really make you laugh, because God started restoring family members in our lives; some members were the ones we prayed for and others we didn't know even existed. As His Word says, He does things completely and more abundantly (Ephesians 3:20). Our small minds cannot even comprehend His thought process (John 10:10).

What a mighty God we serve! How thankful we are to Him! He continued to meet our needs and sustain us, month after month, even when the dollars did not add up, He met the bill payments. During this difficult financial season in my life, there were times I did not have enough money to pay all of my bills, but I remained obedient. I made sure I'd <u>tithe</u> (another tool).

God always blessed the 90 percent I had left, and provided all of my needs and many of my wants. There were times God instructed me to give money to others (which I thought was Crazy!). I just told God, "You will have to make it happen for my bills, because I'm going to do what Your Word says, and I'm going to be obedient." I held on to the Word, which says: "Obedience is better than sacrifice" (1 Samuel 15-22, *NET*) and God just kept keeping me afloat.

God just started showing me that so many people are just barely making it financially, because they do not give their first 10 percent to God (Malachi 3:10). So many of us feel we are giving the money to the Pastor, but we must no longer look at it this way (2 Corinthians 9:7). The fact is, you are giving the money to God, and being **obedient** to His Word. He is the one who will bless you, not the Pastor. You must pray that the shepherd of your church will be obedient to God, and do what God has for him/her to do with the money.

## Journey to Praise

I even saw God work in the court room when a man appearing as Satan scammed one of my nephews. God was the Lawyer and the Judge for my nephew (James 4:12). Initially, it seemed as if my nephew was losing his case, but I kept telling him, "God got you. I don't know how He is going to do it, but just trust Him." The **three** of us (my nephew, a close friend and I) went to court **three** times. Each time we prayed together in the courtroom or at the courtroom's doors. On the **third** court appearance this scammer was arrested, charged with theft by deception, and stayed in jail for **three** days.

It was a miracle right before our eyes and it increased our faith. We were in that courtroom with the **Trinity** (the Father, the Son, and the Holy Ghost). My friend said, "It was like Satan came with Pharaoh's army, but they drowned in the Red Sea." As the Word says, "If God is for us who can be against us" (Romans 8:31, *NIV*) and "No weapon formed against you shall prosper" (Isaiah 54:17, *NKJV*).

## Journey to Praise

Today, the **three** of us still say, the scammer's god did not show up, but our God did appear; showing Himself as who He is, The Great I Am (Exodus 3:14). God says in His Word, "He will never leave us or forsake us" (Deuteronomy 31:8, *NIV*). My nephew ended up getting what the devil stole from him, and now, he has a 'Hallelujah car' too. God our Father, we Praise Your Holy Name! During this court case, we stood on Your tools: **Your Word, praying in numbers, keeping the faith, speaking victory, walking in authority and just watching You, work**. Thank You, God, for the Victory! Hallelujah! Hallelujah! Hallelujah!

My Heavenly Father! My Creator! He led me to join the church that I had been attending. Under my Pastors' spiritual leadership, I learned how to seek God with all of my heart, soul and mind (Deuteronomy 4:29). These Pastors are very spiritually led. The freedom I experienced in this church challenged me to grow in my relationship with God. The Pastors' love for the Lord, and their outpouring spirit through preaching God's Word, helped me during this difficult

## Journey to Praise

time in my life, as I continued to make it through this journey. God used them weekly to give me His Divine Direction. They were used as a catalyst for Him to get to me. I continued to become bold for the Lord and opening my heart for God to use me (Proverbs 28:1).

God continued to work and mold me daily. I asked Him to let my light shine for His glory, and He did (Isaiah 64:8). People within my circle continued to ask me to pray for them; telling me how happy I appeared. The wonder in this observation, they just didn't know that one year ago, I almost lost my mind, everything I owned, and even considered suicide. I felt like such a failure; my spirit was truly broken. "But God," stayed on my mind. I loved Him too much to end my life. This allowed me to continue to seek Him, and trust Him, by using His tools.

My cousin, Cherry, and I continued to pray, and one of our requests was for me to receive the Holy Ghost, the gift of speaking in tongues (Acts 2:1-4). On Pentecost

## Journey to Praise

Sunday 2013, at my church, I was filled with the Holy Ghost. This took my relationship with God to even greater heights and deeper depths. The first **three** days of that week while at work, I silently prayed in tongues. I couldn't stop; I was so excited and filled with the Holy Spirit. Right away, I started seeing God's glory at my job. He continues to shine in my life and push me in new life ventures for Him. Hallelujah! Hallelujah! What a Mighty God I serve!

God has anointed me! Hallelujah!!!!!!!!! Hallelujah!!!!!!!!! Hallelujah!!!!!!!!! He has strengthened my ability to pray. Now I get many inquiries and requests regarding me considering of a career in ministry. I spoke to my two sisters and encouraged a twenty-one day "***Praise Fast***" and prayer. We started the fast on, July 10, 2013, and ended it on, July 30, 2013, which was amazing; it was my one year anniversary from when I had taken a vacation with God. This "Praise Fast" was for breakthroughs, breaking strongholds and for God's overflow in every area of our lives. About

## Journey to Praise

**thirteen** family members and friends joined in this fast.

Twice a week, we held a prayer conference call that was filled with the Holy Spirit (God's presence all in it). Initially, this prayer call started with one of my sister's best friend, asking if I wanted to do a prayer line during our fast. She held other prayer conferences, so she was well equipped to start our prayer call. I replied, "Yes, let's start one." She dedicated a conference line for us to use and I gave the number out to all who were fasting. The **three** of us started facilitating the prayer line (my sister, her friend and me). After our first prayer call, we decided to invite others who weren't fasting. Now we have people calling in from all over the United States praying together (using His tools).

As a result of our prayers and fasting, we witnessed God: (1) Uniting our families (2) Breaking curses (3) Improving our work situations (4) Revealing to us, our life calling (5) Removing all fear (6) Moving and shaking in our lives (shifting the atmosphere). He is blessing us, and we are overwhelmed with His joy and perfect peace.

We have continued our prayer line together on every Tuesday and Thursday (using the tools that God have given us); we have seen many miracles, signs and wonders. We witnessed: babies who were in dying conditions, living; God healing one of our prayer warriors from pancreatic cancer. One prayer warrior's husband received healing from kidney cancer through her intercession on his behalf. We saw God heal hearts of those with heart conditions. The Lord spared an infected finger from being amputated by a physician. He saved houses from foreclosures. He paid seemingly impossible car notes. I saw my church have a huge revival with the presence of God's Shekinah Glory. He gave more years of life to some of our elder family members. This is only a glimpse of what He has done for us. He has opened up doors in our lives that we cannot even explain.

He is continuing to use my family as a vessel for Him. My brother in-law decided to get

## Journey to Praise

ordained, and now he and my sister have their own church. Our prayer line continues to remain obedient, and we were blessed to have our first annual praise/prayer conference at my family's church in Wisconsin. God is breaking chains off of all of us, including anyone near us. He is so faithful, awesome and amazing! God is worthy to be praised!

I now know and believe, it is true; I had to be broken in order for God to use me. He is molding me, right now. He has removed all fear. I have fear of Him and only Him, God my creator. He has given me a spirit of what the Saints call, "The Holy Ghost Boldness." I now realize that I'm a prayer warrior, and that was the reason for me reading the **three** books at the beginning of my consecration.

God continues to speak to me in regards to Peter's walk on the water. He told me, "Peter had the faith of a mustard seed, so even if you get weak I will still save you, just like Peter, who had enough faith to step off the boat and walk on the water." God said,

## Journey to Praise

"Your mustard seed faith is stepping out of your comfort zone, even when you are afraid. It is during your weakness, that I am strong" (2 Corinthians 12:9-10). He also told me, "If I tell you to do something, you must do it, and I will see you through." Hallelujah!!!!! Hallelujah!!!! Praise His Holy Name!!!!!!!!!

About 11 months after my consecration, during my church prayer service, I yielded to God with my hands in the air and eyes closed, yes, with my eyes closed. I saw a bright light shining down on me, and God said, "I have work for you to do." Several months later, He dropped this book in my spirit, to bring forth to the world.

I can truly say God has empowered me through His Holy Spirit. This consecration was a setup. He used this consecration to set me up for victory, success, and to become more prosperous in every area of my life. God showed me a gift I had, one that I didn't know existed. He showed me that it is not about me, it is all about Him; and through Him, I have the <u>Victory</u>. Oh,

# Journey to Praise

how I love Jesus!   Glory! Glory!   Glory! To His Precious Name!

**Now, enough about my journey, let's move forward to yours.**

# Journey to Praise

> *By him therefore let us offer the sacrifice of praise to God continually, that is, the fruit of our lips giving thanks to his name.*
>
> *Hebrews 13:15*

# Journey to Praise

## Your Journey to Praise

### Consecration and Fast

Now, it is time for you to use the <u>tools</u> that God have given **you**. These tools are:

- The fruits of the spirit (Galatians 5:22)
- The gifts of the spirit (1 Corinthians 12:1-31)
- Trust God (Proverbs 3:5-6)
- Read His Word (Matthew 4:4)
- Fast (Luke 5:33)
- Pray fervently without ceasing (1 Thessalonians 5:17)
- Keep a praise on your tongue at all times (Psalms 34:1)
- Walk in authority (2 Peter 1:3)
- Speak life, not death (Proverbs 18:21)
- Put on the full armor of the Lord (Ephesians 6:10-18)
- Tithe, making sure you are giving your ten percent of earnings, and not tipping God (Malachi 3: 8-12)
- Be bold in the Lord (Joshua 1:9)

## Journey to Praise

Begin by consecrating yourself, (separate yourself from others to spend time with God). Let God speak to you. Please, position yourself, so you can hear from Him. Let God's anointing fall down and saturate you. Sacrifice unto the Lord through fasting and prayer for twenty-one days.

This section will provide you with twenty-one praises that will help you to focus on God. I will be praising, praising, praising with you during your journey, as there is power in coming to God in numbers (Matthew 18:20). Please press in and read the scriptures provided during your twenty-one day vacation (The "Praise Fast"). Additionally, the pictures provided are for your enjoyment. They are just some of the many blessings I focused on during my journey.

After you have completed your fast, prayerfully, consider fasting and praying corporately with others on Wednesdays. God is going to change your life. <u>Nothing is impossible for God!</u> This fast is a "Praise Fast." The Word says, God inhabits our praise (Psalms 22:3). Praise will open the

## Journey to Praise

gates of heaven and you will start seeing breakthroughs, God breaking strongholds and God's overflow in your life. While God is all knowing (Job 37:23), a fast increases our faith and our walk with God. During this fast, keep praises on your lips at all time. When the praises go up unto our Savior, His almighty, powerful blessings come down to us.

**Note:** The twenty one praises to follow are inspired by the biblical numbers for each day. Take time each day to journal: your experiences, your feelings and most importantly, what God is doing in your life. Use these daily praise tools to meditate on God and give Him all the praise. God has greatness for you. Press in! Press in! Press in!

# Journey to Praise

## Start your "Praise Fast" with this prayer:

## Prayer

*God, we thank You and Praise You because of who You are. You are the Great I Am. You are God of Gods and Lord of Lords. We thank You for Your Son Jesus Christ and for our salvation. We thank You for the forgiveness of sins. Lord, please forgive us right now. We thank You for the Holy Spirit, our Comforter and Helper. Hallelujah! Heavenly Father, we're coming right now to offer a sacrifice to You. We need Your strength, so we are asking You to release Your Power on us right now. Empower us to be obedient to Your Word and to Your Will. Strengthen us, so we may endure and complete this twenty-one day fast, Father. Lord God, let this fast be life changing for us, now Lord. Cleanse and purify us, Lord. God, we're coming to You with a spirit of expectancy; expecting boundless breakthroughs in our lives, expecting for strongholds to be broken, expecting Your overflow and Your Almighty Gift of Abundance to enter into our lives. Hallelujah! Hallelujah! Hallelujah! We give You All the Praise! We give You All the Glory! We give You All the Honor! In Your Precious Son's Name, Jesus the Christ, we pray. Amen! Amen! Amen!*

# Journey to Praise

1. Praise God for Day One of the Fast (Unity-New Beginnings). He is going to do a new thing in our lives. This is our start to a new beginning. We are seeking to be complete, in Your will and in Your way. This is our new season! Lord, we want Your divine restoration. Lord, transform us! Renew us! Hallelujah! Hallelujah! To the most high! Lord, You are Worthy to be Praised!!!!!!!!!!!!!!!!!!!!!!!!!
*Isaiah 42:9-10, Isaiah 43:18-19*

# Journey to Praise

## Day One

Journal:

# Journey to Praise

# Journey to Praise

2. Day Two of Fast (Union). Hallelujah! Hallelujah! Let us fast today keeping our minds focused on God. Let us seek His face; knowing He is the Only True and Living God. We are collectively standing on His Word, and it says, "Ask and it will be given to you; seek and you will find; knock and the door will be opened to you. For everyone who asks receives; the one who seeks finds; and to the one who knocks, the door will be opened" (Matthew 7:7-8, *NET)*. God, we are asking for the chains to be removed; let the shackles fall now! Give us wisdom! Thank You, Jesus!! Cleanse us! Renew us! Refresh us! Restore us! We sacrifice unto You, Lord! We thank You for all Your many blessings! Hallelujah! Hallelujah! Thank You, God!!!!!!!!!!!!!
*Deuteronomy 4:29-31, Matthew 21:21, 1 John 5:14-15*

# Journey to Praise

## Day Two

Journal:

# Journey to Praise

# Journey to Praise

3. Day Three of Fast (Trinity). Praise the Father, Son & Holy Spirit. Get ready for miracles, signs and wonders. Jesus rose from the dead in **three** days. In the Bible, **three** men (Shadrach, Meshach, and Abednego) were in the fiery furnace; they lived, and did not die. Just know that your trials and tribulations are only molding you. God is taking you to another level. Prepare for your breakthroughs, breaking of strongholds & receiving God's overflow. As Bishop T.D. Jakes would say: "Get Ready! Get Ready! Get Ready!!!!!!!!!!!!!!!!!!!!!!!!!!!!!!!!!!!!!!!!!!!!!!!!!!!
*Hebrews 2:1-4, Romans 15:14-21, Daniel 3:13-30*

# Journey to Praise

## Day Three

Journal:

# Journey to Praise

# Journey to Praise

4. Day Four of Fast (A *Day of Creation*). Let us creatively Praise God today. Shout unto the Lord! Sing unto the Lord! Lift our hands up unto the Lord! Dance unto the Lord! He is the Almighty God. He made the heaven and the earth. He is our Creator. Let God create the calling in you that He has for your life. Praise Him! Praise Him! Praise Him! He is worthy to be praised! Hallelujah! Hallelujah!!!!!!!!!!!!!!!!!!!!!
*Genesis 1:1-2, Exodus 15:2, Acts 13:22, Psalms 7:17, Psalms 9:2*

# Journey to Praise

## Day Four

Journal:

# Journey to Praise

# Journey to Praise

5. Fast-Day Five (A *Day of Grace*). God is giving us life in abundance, more than what we deserve. Let's keep Pressing towards the Mark of The High Calling. Read His Word, pray, and have faith. Amen! Amen! Amen!!!!!!!!!!!!!!!!!!!!!!!!!!!!!!!!!!!!
*Acts 17:11, John 1:14-18, Romans 3:21-24, Philippians 3:14-15*

# Journey to Praise

## Day Five

Journal:

# Journey to Praise

# Journey to Praise

6. Fast-Day Six (A D*ay of Weakness)*.  Let us cry out, now, to our Father for His Strength.  Lord God, we need Your help.  We need Your Strength.  Lord, carry us through this fast and make us whole.  We want to be more like Jesus.  Release Your power, God!  Reveal Your glory, Lord!  You are Alpha and Omega, the First and the Last, the Beginning and the End!  Glory Hallelujah, Lord!!!!!!!!!!!!!!!!!!!!!!!!!!!!!!!!!!!!!!!!!!!!!!!!!!!!!!
*Isaiah 41:10, Philippians 4:13, 2 Timothy 4:17, 1 Peter 4:1*

# Journey to Praise

## Day Six

Journal:

# Journey to Praise

# Journey to Praise

7. Hallelujah! Hallelujah! Day Seven of Fast (A *Day of Completion*). God honors us when we complete our accomplishments. Our victory is in reach, just reach out and grab it.
Victory! Victory! Victory!!!!!!!!!!!!!!!!!!!!!!!!!!!!!!!
*James 1:1-4, Philippians 1:4-6, Matthew 13:36-43*

# Journey to Praise

## Day Seven

Journal:

# Journey to Praise

## Journey to Praise

8. Fast-Day Eight (A day of *New Beginnings*). God wants to do something new in our lives, something great! We just need to give up something or someone. We need to start anew and seek God's face. Everything we want and need is in HIM. It is written, "Obedience is better than sacrifice" (1 Samuel 15:22, *NET*). Praise The Lord! Trust The Lord! Amen! Amen! Amen!!!!!!!!!
*Proverbs 3:5-6, 2 Corinthians 12:9, 2 Timothy 1:7*

# Journey to Praise

## Day Eight

Journal:

# Journey to Praise

# Journey to Praise

9. Fast-Day Nine (A Day of "Fruit"). This fruit comes from God; because the fruit of the spirit is God (love, joy, peace, forbearance, kindness, goodness, faithfulness, gentleness, and self-control). Let your fruit shine, so you can bring the lost to our Lord and Savior. Get more in tune with God's purpose for your life. Let it shine! Let it shine! Let it shine!!!!!!!!!!!!!!!!!!!!!!!!!!!!!!!!!!!!!!!!
*Galatians 5:22-23, James 1:22, Proverbs 19:21, Exodus 9:16*

# Journey to Praise

## Day Nine

Journal:

# Journey to Praise

# Journey to Praise

10. Hallelujah! Day Ten of Fast (A *Day of Testimony*). Let us rejoice in the Lord for what He has done for us. Let us share with our neighbors, so that they may have hope. If God did it for us, He can do it for them! If He did it for me, He can do it for you! "God is no respecter of persons" (Acts 10:34). Praise His Holy Name!!!!!!!!!!!!!!!!!!!!!!!!!
*2 Timothy 18, Revelation 12:11, Luke 8:39, Psalms 119:4*

## Journey to Praise

## Day Ten

Journal:

# Journey to Praise

# Journey to Praise

11. Fast-Day Eleven (A *Day of Judgment*). God Almighty is the only to judge. He is our Redeemer, for He loves justice. He is our lawyer in the courtroom. He never lets the guilty go unpunished. We must just trust the Lord, Our God. We Trust You! We Trust You, Lord!!!!!!!!!!!!
*Matthew 7:1-5, James 4:11-12, Psalms 10:17-18, Isaiah 42:3-4, Psalms 43:1*

# Journey to Praise

Day Eleven

Journal:

# Journey to Praise

# Journey to Praise

12. Fast-Day Twelve (A *Day of Perfection*). Let us pray for our leaders. Let them lead through God's will. Let us strive for excellence and do what is pleasing to God, our Lord and Savior. Glory to God. Press! Press! Press!!!!!!!!!!!!!!!!!!!!!!!!!!!!!!! *Matthew 5:48, James 1:4, 2 Corinthians 13:9, Colossians 3:14*

# Journey to Praise

## Day Twelve

Journal:

# Journey to Praise

# Journey to Praise

13. Fast-Day Thirteen (A Day of Lawlessness). This is the *day the Lord has made*, let us rejoice and be glad in it. We are soldiers for the Lord, and it is time to put on the full armor of the Lord. We are fighting against principalities. Pray for your enemy. God says, "Vengeance is mine" (Romans 12:19). We are touching and agreeing, standing on His Word, the Truth. Keep standing! Keep Standing! If God is for us, who can be against us! Bless Your Name, Lord!   Bless Your Name! Hallelujah!!!!!!!!!!!!!!!!!!!!!!!!!!!!!!!!!!!!!!!!!!!!!!
*Ephesians 6:10-18, Acts 17:11, Ephesians 6:11, Romans 12:19, Proverbs 24:29*

# Journey to Praise

## Day Thirteen

Journal:

# Journey to Praise

# Journey to Praise

14. Hallelujah! Fast-Day Fourteen (A *Day of Deliverance and Salvation*). Jesus is our Deliverer, Redeemer, Provider, Protector, Helper, and Our Everything. How grateful we are to Him. Let each of us, collectively, put on the helmet of salvation. The victory is already ours. Thanks Be To God! Let us all give HIM Thanks!!!!!!!!!!!!!!!!!!
*1 Thessalonians 1:10, Psalms 56:13,*
  *Romans 3:23, Psalms 91:2-3, Ecclesiastes 7:26*

# Journey to Praise

## Day Fourteen

Journal:

# Journey to Praise

# Journey to Praise

15. Fast-Day Fifteen (A *Day of Rest*).  God says in His Word, to give our worries, our burdens, and our battles to Him, and He will carry us.  Let us all go now and rest in His peace, His joy, and His strength.  It is written, "Peace be Still," says the Lord (Mark 4:39, *NKJV*).  Rest also means to trust God, so let us trust Him and only Him.  Let us be still and yield to God, so we can hear from Him, for His Divine Direction.  Go in peace and serve the Lord!   Thanks be to God! Amen! Amen! Amen!!!!!!!!!!!!!!!!!!!!!!!!!!!!!!!!!!!!!!!!!!!!!!!!!!!!
*Exodus 33:14, Matthew 11:28-30, John 14:25-27, Mark 6:31, Isaiah 57:1-2*

# Journey to Praise

## Day Fifteen

Journal:

# Journey to Praise

# Journey to Praise

16. Fast-Day Sixteen (A *Day of Love*). Jesus is Love! Jesus loved us first. God loved us so much; He sent His only Son to die for us on the cross, for the forgiveness of all of our sins. There is no greater love than His love. Let us rejoice in His love and show His love to others. Let us love our neighbors as ourselves, even our enemies; for loving our enemy is the true test. Let's pass the test and Love! Love! Love! Let your light shine! We are more than conquerors! Hallelujah! Glory to His name!!!!!!!!!!!!!!!!!!!!!!!!!!!!!!!!!!!!!!!!!!!!!!
*Ephesians 5:2, Romans 12:10, Deuteronomy 6:5, 1 John 4:8*

# Journey to Praise

## Day Sixteen

Journal:

# Journey to Praise

# Journey to Praise

17. Fast-Day Seventeen (A *Day of Victory*). We are close to completing our fast. Victory is already ours. Breakthroughs are happening. God is breaking strongholds. We have the Victory of overflow and God's gift of abundance. Get up and walk in authority. You have to know who your "Daddy" is, to know the power we have. Tap into His power, His love, His tools, and He will let you know the battle is already won. Have that Faith of the mustard seed. Victory is yours! Victory is mine! Victory is ours today! Go in peace and serve The Lord! Hallelujah! Hallelujah! Hallelujah!!!!!!!!!!!!!!!!!!!!!!!!!!!!!!!!!!!!!!!!!!!!!!!!
*Revelations 12:11, Deuteronomy 20:4,*
*2 Chronicles 7:14, Psalms 3:8, Joshua 10:8*

# Journey to Praise

## Day Seventeen

Journal:

# Journey to Praise

# Journey to Praise

18. Fast-Day Eighteen (A *Day of Bondage*). In God, there is no more bondage. No more bondage financially; no more bondage in sickness; no more bondage in relationships; no more bondage at work; no more bondage mentally; no more bondage in addictions, no more bondage physically; and no more bondage to our enemy. Hallelujah! Hallelujah! Through the blood of Jesus, we have been set free. We are pleading the blood of Jesus over our lives, right now. God, we thank You for loving us so much. We do not have enough tongues to say, Thank You, Lord! We just want to say Thank You, Lord! Glory to the Most High!!!!!!!!!!!!!!!!!!!!!!!!!!!!!!!!!!!!!!!!!!!!!!
*Romans 8:15, Hebrews 2:14-15, 2 Peter 2:17-19, John 8:34-36*

# Journey to Praise

## Day Eighteen

Journal:

# Journey to Praise

# Journey to Praise

19. Fast-Day Nineteen (A D*ay of Faith)*. Praise the Lord. The Word says, " Truly I tell you, if anyone says to this mountain, Go, throw yourself into the sea, and does not doubt in their heart but believes that what they say will happen, it will be done for them" (Matthew 11:23, *NIV*). We build our faith through reading the Word, it is not by sight. Where is our faith in God? We just need the faith of the mustard seed. It can knock the walls down; it can open up the sea; it can save us in the burning furnace; it can save us in the lion's den; it can save us from the flood; and it can let us walk on water. Look to God and not your problem. Have that faith of the mustard seed and God will carry you through. We speak to that mountain and say, move, move, and move. Glory to God! If God tells you to do it, step out and do it. Let us keep looking forward and not behind. Look forward to God. Forward! Forward! Forward! Hallelujah! Hallelujah!!!!!!!!!!!!!!!!!!!!!!!!
*1 Corinthians 16:13, Titus 1:2, Psalms 23,*
*Matthew 17:20, Hebrews 11:1, Matthew 21:21*

# Journey to Praise

## Day Nineteen

Journal:

# Journey to Praise

# Journey to Praise

20. Fast-day Twenty (A *Day of Redemption*). Glory to God! Thank You, Lord, for saving us. You didn't have to do it, but You did it anyhow. You didn't give up on us, despite of our sins. You sent Your Son, Christ Jesus, to save us, to deliver us, and to redeem us. Hallelujah! Now we have the greatest gift of all, eternal life with You. We have the gift of You, delivering us from bad situations, bad thoughts, and all problems in our lives. Your Word says, we will face problems; however, You will walk with us and never leave us. Hallelujah!!
*Ephesians 1:7, Galatians 2:20, Colossians 1:14, Titus 2:14*

# Journey to Praise

## Day Twenty

Journal:

# Journey to Praise

# Journey to Praise

21. Fast-Day Twenty-One (A Day which is a Multiple of Seven). Hallelujah! Hallelujah! Hallelujah! We thank God for completing **three** weeks (21 days) of sacrificing to Our Father, The Son, & The Holy Spirit. Thank You, Lord, for breakthroughs, breaking strongholds & sending Your overflow. Thank You, God, for miracles, signs & wonders. We believe, we receive, and through You, we will achieve. We will go now as new creatures, looking forward, expecting to live new, see new, and be new, in Christ. Lord, we are expecting to have changed lives. We are expecting You, Lord, to take us to places in our lives we have never been, but could only go with YOU. We are free indeed! We have won! We will not stop Pressing! Victory! Victory! Victory! Victory is ours! Hallelujah, Lord! Hallelujah!!!!!!!!!!!!!!!!!!!!
*Romans 12:1, 1 John 2:2, Hosea 6:6, 1 John 4:10, Hebrews 13:15*

# Journey to Praise

## Day Twenty-One

Journal:

# Journey to Praise

# Journey to Praise

## End the Praise Fast with this prayer:

## Prayer

*Thank You, Lord! Thank You, Lord! We love You, Lord! God, we thank You, Lord, for keeping us during this twenty-one day fast, and allowing us to come humbly before You, Lord. Lord, thank You, for Your sweet presence showing up and always showing up on time. You are a timely God. Thank You, Lord, for Your deliverance during this fast and for You being our Redeemer. Lord, we thank You for the gift of Your precious Son, Jesus, and the gift of eternal life. Cleanse and purify us right now; renew us from the sins that we have committed. Lord, thank You for allowing us to spend this precious time getting to know You better, and getting closer to You. We know there is nothing that we cannot accomplish, as long as we use the tools You have provided, Lord. Thank You, for Your tools (Your Word-the Bible, faith, praise, prayer, tithing, walking in Your authority, fasting, and using the fruits/gifts of the Holy Spirit). Continue to work through us and on us. Empower us, so we will do what is of Your will and what is pleasing in Your sight. God, let our lights shine, so all who we encounter will notice something different about us. We want to share that it is the Jesus inside of us that they see. Hallelujah! Thank You, Lord, for Breakthroughs, Breaking Strongholds and Overflow. We ask all of these things in the Name of Your Son, Jesus Christ. Amen! Amen! Amen!*

# Journey to Praise

You have the victory. Go in peace and serve the Lord! Continue to keep your mind on Jesus. Remember, you live in this world, but you are not of this world (2 Corinthians 10:3). Share your testimonies with others, letting them know what God is doing in your life after your fast, and after this supernatural change in your life. If God did it for you, He will do it for your friends and your family.

God has so much for all of us, we just need to know how to **tap** into His power, and now you have tapped in. Do not stop, keep pressing forward. **God has a calling on your life; we all just need to have faith, and make ourselves available to Him.**

*Are you just too busy that you do not give time to God?* Keep fasting and praying (using the tools) throughout the year and fasting on Wednesdays. Get others to join in with you, remembering, there is power in numbers. I'm so excited with what God is about to do in your life. To God Be the Glory!

# Journey to Praise

> *For God so loved the world, that he gave his only begotten Son, that whosoever believeth in him should not perish, but have everlasting life.*
>
> *John 3:16*

# Journey to Praise

## Journey Continues

## ***Special Bonus***

Praises (tools) for the Wednesday Fasts or for, however, you choose to use them to glorify God:

1. Praise God! It is our day of sacrifice unto our Lord and Savior. Let God's anointing fill us now. Lord, cleanse us, so that we can come humbly before our King. Our lives will never be the same. We believe in Your supernatural powers. We expect to see miracles, signs, and wonders. Open the windows of heaven and pour Your blessings down on us, Lord! We have hope in You. Fill us up, Lord! Fill us up! Thank You, Lord!!!!!!!!!!!!!!!!!!!!!!!!!!!!!!!!!!
*Malachi 3:10, 2 Corinthians 12:12, Romans 15:19*

**Journal:**

_____
_____
_____
_____

## Journey to Praise

2. God, we are crying out to You. Help! Help! Help us, we are Your children. We, collectively, come before You, honoring You, offering our sacrifices unto You. Make us whole, Lord. Change our lives, Lord. Lead us and guide us. Give us pure hearts. We have great expectations of Your Superiority, of Your Power. How Great You Are! Show us, Lord! Show us, Lord! We love You, Lord! Thank You, Jesus!!!!!!!!!!!!!!!
*Psalms 5:2, Psalms 57:2, Psalms 51:10*

**Journal:**

_____

_____

_____

_____

_____

3. Glory! Glory! Hallelujah! You are a Wonder, Lord! You're a Wonder! We come before You, Lord, offering everything we have. We fast before You today, Lord. You are our Great Jehovah and there is no other. We offer up unto You, our worship, Lord. We offer up

## Journey to Praise

unto You, all of our praises, Lord. You're worthy, Lord! You're worthy! We surrender, Lord! We surrender!!!!
*Matthew 7:11, John 17:26, Psalms 72:18-19, Ezekiel 11:22, Psalms 103:11-14, Deuteronomy 4:39*

**Journal:**

_____
_____
_____
_____
_____
_____
_____

4. Oh God! Oh God! You are so Wonderful! You are more precious than gold and sweeter than honey. You're beautiful, Lord! We just cannot express how much joy we have in You, Lord. We each come giving of what we have unto You. We magnify You, Lord! We lift up holy hands unto You! You are worthy to be Praised! Glory to Your Name! Glory to Your Name!!!!!!!!!!!!!
*Psalms 19:10, Proverbs 8:11, Psalms 134:2*

# Journey to Praise

**Journal:**

_____
_____
_____
_____
_____

5. Father, we love You because of who You are. We are sacrificing unto You, asking You to open our hearts, Lord. Lord, open our eyes up unto You, Father. Let us seek Your face, Lord. Let us work at being more like You, Jesus. Let our path be straight and not crooked, Lord. Lord, let us be led by the spirit and not by the mind, Father. God, show us the way. Lord, show us the light. We will follow You, Lord! We will follow! Hallelujah! Hallelujah!!!!!!!!
*Psalms 27:8, Deuteronomy 4:29, Lamentations 3:25, Matthew 6:33, Psalms 105:4*

**Journal:**

_____
_____

## Journey to Praise

_____
_____

6. Hallelujah! Hallelujah! Empower us, Lord, with wisdom. We know our help come from You, Lord. Lord God, impart Your favor on us right now, Father. We humbly give ourselves sacrificing unto You, Lord. Have mercy on us, Lord! Have mercy on us, Lord! Praise Your Name! Praise Your Holy Name, Jesus!! *2 Chronicles 1:10-12, Ecclesiastes 7:25, Proverbs 15:12, Matthew 7:24*

**Journal:**

_____
_____
_____
_____
_____
_____

7. Heavenly Father, we thank You, Lord! Thank You, Lord, for strengthening us for another day. Father, we know we have work to do, kingdom work, for we

## Journey to Praise

are Your servants. We preach Jesus Christ as Lord. God, we give of ourselves to You. Lord, use us and fill our hearts with Your light. To God Be the Glory! Hallelujah! Hallelujah!!!!!!!!!!!
*John 13:35, Matthew 28:19-20, Acts 2:1-47*

**Journal:**

_____

_____

_____

_____

_____

_____

8. Praise Your Name, Father! Praise Your Name! Thank You, Lord, for we know nothing can separate us from Your Love! Thank You, Lord, for loving us first, Father. Thank You, for loving us so much. We know we have the victory through You. Hallelujah! Hallelujah! We offer up unto You everything we have, Father. We Love You, Lord! We Love You!!!!!!!!!!!!!!!!!!!!!!!!!!!!!!!!!!
*Romans 8:31-39*

# Journey to Praise

**Journal:**

_____
_____
_____
_____
_____
_____

9. Oh God, we thank You that You are near and dear to our hearts. We worship You! We praise You! We lift Your Name up, Jesus, unto all! During this time of sacrifice, please continue to increase our faith. We know we cannot please You without faith, Lord. We know that when we call out unto You, You save us. Hallelujah! Glory! Glory! Hallelujah!!!!!!!!!!!!!!!!!!!!!!!!!!!!!!!!!!
*1 John 3:21, Hebrews 10:22*

**Journal:**

_____
_____
_____
_____

## Journey to Praise

10. Dear Father in Heaven, we thank You for Your mercy and Your grace. Thank You, Lord, for putting us right with You. Thank You, Lord, for Your blood. Thank You, Lord, for being our friend. God, we rejoice before You, Lord. You are our Almighty God. Purge us and cleanse us, so we can come humbly before You today, offering of ourselves. We sacrifice unto You! We sacrifice! We Love You, Lord!!!!!!!!!!!!!!!!!!!!!!!!!!!!!
*Hebrews 11:6, Romans 5:1, Ecclesiastes 3:11*

**Journal:**

# Journey to Praise

Never stop using the tools our Lord and Savior have given you. Remember, **praise, prayer, fasting, the Word, faith, tithing, walking in God's authority, the armor of the Lord, the gifts and fruits of the spirit**, are what you need to walk through your journey to be successful in this world.

I have learned throughout my journey, it is all in how gracefully you handle the situation, as this will allow you to see God's grace in all things. Keep on pressing forward. Pressing towards the Mark of the High Calling (Philippians 3:14). Glory to God! The Most High!

I love you with God's love!
(Colossians 3:12-17)

Your Sister In Christ,

Jackie